BEYOND MASTERING: TECHNIQUES FOR TIME, TEAM, AND SELF-MANAGEMENT

Elevating Your Management Game

Steven Bradley

CONTENTS

ELEVATING YOUR MANAGEMENT GAME

In today's fast-paced and ever-evolving business landscape, being an effective manager requires more than just overseeing tasks and ensuring deadlines are met. The demands of modern leadership call for advanced strategies that go beyond the basics of time management and team coordination. Whether you're leading a small team, managing a large organization, or navigating the complexities of remote and hybrid work, your ability to adapt, innovate, and inspire is crucial to achieving success in your role.

This is a follow-up to my first book, *"Not Me, Not Now, Managing Your Time, Your Team, and Yourself,"* and is designed to help you elevate your management skills to the next level. It is not just about doing more; it's about doing better—maximizing efficiency, fostering a positive and productive work environment, and ultimately driving your team toward success in a sustainable and meaningful way. The chapters that follow cover advanced management techniques, each aimed at providing you with the tools and insights necessary to thrive in today's complex business world. Be sure to check out the References & Resources section at the back for where to find more on some of the topics covered.

We begin with "Chapter One: Beyond Lists: Organizational Strategies," where you'll learn how to refine your organizational skills with sophisticated techniques that go beyond traditional to-do lists. From task decomposition to prioritization matrices, this chapter will equip you with the methods needed to streamline your workflow and enhance your productivity.

In "Chapter Two: The 9-Minute Rule: Planning Efficiency," we explore how dedicating just nine minutes a day to focused planning can revolutionize your approach to managing tasks and goals. This chapter will guide you through the strategies that can help you optimize your planning process, ensuring that every minute counts.

"Chapter Three: The Prioritization Matrix: A Deeper Dive," takes you further into the art of prioritization. Here, you'll discover how to handle competing priorities and urgent tasks with precision, using proven frameworks that help you focus on what truly matters.

Delegation is a key skill for any manager, and in "Chapter Four: Delegation Mastery: Not Me, Not Now in Action," we explore advanced delegation techniques. You'll learn how to empower your team, distribute tasks effectively, and maintain control without micromanaging.

As a leader, it's not enough to respond to challenges as they arise; you must anticipate them. "Chapter Five: Proactive Leadership: Anticipating Challenges," provides you with the tools to foresee potential obstacles and address them before they impact your team's performance.

Every team is unique, and so is every management situation. "Chapter Six: Tailoring Management Styles: One Size Doesn't Fit All," offers insights into how to adapt your management style to fit different team members and situations, balancing flexibility with consistency.

The rise of remote and hybrid work environments has changed the way we lead. In "Chapter Seven: Virtual Leadership: A New Reality," you'll find best practices for leading in this new normal, along with strategies for maintaining engagement and productivity across dispersed teams.

The roles of a coach, mentor, and manager are distinct, yet they often overlap. "Chapter Eight: Coaching vs. Mentoring vs. Managing: Applied Techniques," provides a deep dive into these different roles, helping you determine when and how to apply each approach for maximum impact.

Sustainability is not just about environmental stewardship; it's about ensuring long-term success in every aspect of management. "Chapter Nine: Sustainability in Management: Long-Term Success," offers strategies for balancing short-term goals with a long-term vision, ensuring that your leadership is both effective and sustainable.

In a rapidly changing world, the ability to adapt is crucial. "Chapter Ten: The Evolving Manager: Adapting to Change," focuses on how to stay relevant and effective, with techniques for continuous learning and self-improvement.

Finally, in "Chapter Eleven: Networking and Influence: Your Professional Brand," we explore the importance of networking in building your professional brand. You'll learn advanced strategies for expanding your network and leveraging it for career growth and opportunities.

As you journey through this book, you'll find that the principles and practices outlined are not just theoretical concepts but actionable strategies that you can implement immediately. The goal is to equip you with the knowledge and tools to become a more effective, adaptable, and influential leader —one who is prepared to meet the challenges of today's dynamic business environment head-on.

Welcome to a new level of management mastery.

ONE: BEYOND LISTS. ORGANIZATIONAL STRATEGIES

C reating and managing to-do lists is more than just jotting down tasks on a piece of paper. Advanced techniques involve breaking down larger tasks into smaller, more manageable actions. This method, known as task decomposition, helps in visualizing the steps needed to complete a project, making it less overwhelming and more achievable. By specifying subtasks, you can track progress more accurately and stay motivated as you tick off each item.

In this chapter, we will discuss methods and techniques helpful in managing your tasks.

Prioritization is another crucial element in advanced to-do list management. I was using a method to prioritize activities for many years, and

I didn't even know where I learned it or what it was called. It turned out to be a modified version of the Eisenhower Matrix.[1] The Eisenhower Matrix, a powerful prioritization tool, divides tasks into four categories based on urgency and importance. By categorizing tasks into "Do First, Schedule, Delegate, and Don't Do," you can apply a strategy that helps you focus on what truly matters and avoid getting bogged down by less critical activities. This method ensures you allocate your time and energy to tasks that align with your goals and deliver the most value.

Time-blocking is an effective technique that pairs well with to-do lists. You create a structured schedule that enhances focus and productivity by assigning specific time slots to tasks. This method helps in managing your time efficiently, reducing the tendency to procrastinate, and ensuring that important tasks receive the attention they deserve. Combining time-blocking with prioritized to-do lists creates an effective system for managing your day.

Regular review and adjustment of your to-do lists are essential for maintaining their effectiveness. Daily and weekly reviews allow you to assess progress, reprioritize tasks, and adapt to changing circumstances. This practice helps in identifying completed tasks, shifting deadlines, and ensuring that your list remains relevant and aligned with your objectives. It also provides an opportunity for reflection and continuous improvement in your organizational strategies.

Incorporating flexibility into your to-do lists is vital. Life is unpredictable, and rigid lists can lead to frustration when things don't go as planned. By building buffer times and allowing for adjustments, you can create a more realistic and adaptable plan. This approach helps in managing unexpected events and maintaining a sense of control over your schedule, leading to better overall productivity.

Tools And Apps To Enhance Productivity

Technology offers a plethora of tools and apps designed to enhance productivity and streamline task management. I have used several different tools over the years and as I was preparing for this book, I discovered a few more. One of the most popular apps is Todoist,[P1] which provides a robust platform for creating, organizing, and prioritizing tasks. While I don't have a lot of experience with this tool, I found its interface and powerful features, such as project categorization and due date assignment, make it suitable for productivity enthusiasts. Todoist also integrates with other tools like Google Calendar and Slack, enhancing its functionality and making it a central hub for task management.

Another highly recommended tool, and one I have used extensively, is Trello,[p2] known for its visual approach to task management. Trello uses boards, lists, and cards to represent projects and tasks, providing a clear and intuitive way to track progress. This app is particularly useful for collaborative projects, allowing team members to assign tasks, set deadlines, and communicate within the platform. Trello's flexibility and ease of use make it a versatile tool for both personal and professional use.

Jira, by Atlassian,[p3] is a powerful project management tool that offers advanced features for organizing tasks and tracking team performance. With Jira, you can create detailed project plans, assign tasks to team members, and set priorities and deadlines. Its timeline and workload features provide a comprehensive view of project progress and resource allocation. Jira's ability to integrate with various other tools, such as Slack, Microsoft Teams, and Google Drive, enhances its functionality and makes it an essential tool for complex projects.

For those who prefer a minimalist approach, Microsoft To Do[p4] offers a straightforward and efficient way to manage tasks. A simple interface allows users to create lists, set reminders, and organize tasks with ease. The integration with Microsoft 365 applications, such as Outlook and OneNote, provides a seamless experience for users who are already within the Microsoft ecosystem. Microsoft To Do's focus on simplicity and functionality makes it a great choice for individuals looking for a no-frills task management solution.

Evernote,[P5] while primarily known as a note-taking app, also excels in task management. With features like notebooks, tags, and reminders, Evernote allows you to organize tasks and related information in a highly customizable way. Its powerful search capabilities make it easy to find specific notes and tasks, even in extensive collections. Evernote's ability to store and organize various types of information, from text notes to web clippings and attachments, makes it a versatile tool for comprehensive task management and productivity enhancement.

These examples of task management tools are certainly not an exhaustive one. Many of the apps out there use similar features and functions, this allows you to adjust to changes in your job or the availability of a specific app given your circumstance. Be sure to take some time to research a few to better understand which ones fit your style, your team, and your organization.

Also, check out the References & Resources section of this book for more information.

Combining Techniques And Tools For Optimal Productivity

The key to maximizing productivity lies in combining advanced techniques with the right tools. For instance, using Trello's visual boards in conjunction with the Eisenhower Matrix can help you prioritize tasks effectively. By creating lists that categorize tasks based on urgency and importance, you can visualize your priorities and allocate your time more efficiently. This combination ensures that you focus on high-impact tasks while keeping track of less critical ones.

Integrating time-blocking with digital tools like Todoist or Microsoft To Do can also enhance productivity. By assigning specific time slots to tasks within these apps, you create a structured schedule that promotes focus and accountability. Most of these tools offer features to set due dates and reminders, ensuring that you stay on track with your time-blocking plan. This integration helps in maintaining a disciplined approach to task management and reducing procrastination.

Collaboration tools like Jira and Trello are invaluable for team-based projects. These platforms allow team members to assign tasks, set deadlines, and communicate within the app, promoting transparency and accountability. By using these tools, teams can manage projects more efficiently, track progress in real-time, and ensure that everyone is aligned with the project goals. This collaborative approach enhances productivity and fosters a sense of shared responsibility.

Regularly reviewing and adjusting your task management system is crucial for long-term success. Combining daily and weekly reviews with digital tools allows you to track progress, identify bottlenecks, and make necessary adjustments. Tools like Evernote can be used to store review notes and action plans, providing a centralized repository for continuous improvement. This practice ensures that your system remains dynamic and responsive to changing needs and priorities.

Integrating flexibility into your task management approach is essential. Tools like Trello and Jira offer features to move tasks between lists and adjust deadlines, providing the flexibility needed to adapt to unexpected changes.

By using these features, you can maintain a realistic and adaptable task management system that accommodates the unpredictability of daily life. This approach helps in reducing stress and maintaining a sense of control over your schedule, ultimately enhancing overall productivity.

TWO: THE 9-MINUTE RULE. PLANNING EFFICIENCY

Effective planning is the cornerstone of productivity, and the 9-Minute Rule is designed to maximize efficiency in this critical area. In my first book I presented the idea of dedicating just nine minutes each day to planning, where you can create a roadmap that guides your actions and priorities. This brief but focused planning session helps you clarify your goals, identify key tasks, and allocate your time effectively. The key to success lies in maintaining extreme focus during these nine minutes, ensuring that every second is used purposefully.

Daily planning involves setting aside a few minutes each morning to outline your tasks and goals for the day. Start by reviewing your to-do list and prioritizing tasks based on urgency and importance. The Eisenhower Matrix can be a useful tool here, helping you categorize tasks and focus on what truly matters. Use your nine minutes to break down larger tasks into manageable steps, allocate specific time slots for each activity, and set reminders to keep yourself on track. This practice ensures that you begin each day with a clear plan and a focused mindset.

Weekly planning extends this concept to a broader timeframe, allowing you to align your daily tasks with longer-term goals. Spend time at the start or end of each week to review your progress, set priorities for the coming days, and adjust your schedule as needed. This session should include a review of your calendar, identification of key deadlines, and allocation of time for important projects. By maintaining extreme focus during this session, you can ensure that your weekly plan is comprehensive and realistic, setting the stage for a productive week.

Monthly planning takes a high-level view of your goals and objectives, allowing you to align your activities with your broader vision. Dedicate time at the beginning or end of each month to reflect on your achievements, identify areas for improvement, and set new goals. This session should include a review of your long-term projects, deadlines, and milestones. Use this time to adjust your plans based on progress and changing priorities. By focusing intently during this planning session, you can ensure that your monthly plan serves as a solid foundation for your weekly and daily activities.

Incorporating extreme focus into your planning sessions is crucial for maximizing their effectiveness. Eliminate distractions, find a quiet space, and commit to using the full time you've allocated for planning without interruptions. This level of concentration helps you make better decisions, prioritize tasks more effectively, and create plans that are both actionable and aligned with your goals. By adopting this approach, you can transform your planning sessions into powerful tools for productivity and success.

Case Studies On Successful Planning Habits

Several successful individuals and organizations have harnessed the power of effective planning to achieve remarkable results. One notable example is Elon Musk, CEO of Tesla and SpaceX, who is known for his meticulous planning habits. Musk uses a time-blocking method to allocate his time in five-minute increments,[2] ensuring that each task receives focused attention. By planning his day down to the minute, he maximizes productivity and maintains extreme focus on his priorities. While I find this approach a bit excessive, who am I to question Musk's results as this has enabled him to juggle multiple high-stakes projects and drive innovation in various industries.[3]

Another case study, and one that I am intimately familiar with, involves the team at IBM, renowned for its methodical and structured approach to project management and innovation. IBM employees leverage the IBM Design Thinking[4] framework, which combines agile methodologies with user-centered design principles. This framework encourages iterative development and collaboration across teams, with a focus on solving complex problems efficiently. IBM also uses agile sprints to break down larger initiatives into manageable tasks and incorporates key performance indicators (KPIs) to measure success and progress. This approach has enabled IBM to consistently drive innovation and maintain its position as a leader in the technology sector.

I remember fondly when I bought my first Franklin Planner. [p6] Paired with a multi-color ink pen, (yeah, I'm that old), I had planning organized and color-coded. It was a game-changer for me!

The story of FranklinCovey, a global consulting firm specializing in productivity and time management, also highlights the importance of effective planning. The company's founder, Stephen R. Covey authored the bestselling book "The 7 Habits of Highly Effective People," which emphasizes the role of planning in personal and professional success. FranklinCovey's planners and time management systems, such as the Franklin Planner, are designed to help individuals prioritize tasks, set goals, and maintain extreme focus. These tools have been widely adopted by individuals and organizations seeking to enhance their productivity.

So, if you'd rather minimize your screen time and avoid using technology, go check out a Franklin Planner!

Lastly, the story of Michael Hyatt, a bestselling author and leadership coach, demonstrates the power of effective planning in personal development. Hyatt advocates for the use of the Full Focus Planner,[P7] a tool he designed to help individuals set and achieve their goals. The planner incorporates daily, weekly, and monthly planning sessions, encouraging users to maintain extreme focus and align their activities with their long-term vision. Hyatt's approach has helped thousands of individuals enhance their productivity and achieve their goals.

These case studies highlight the transformative impact of effective planning. By dedicating just nine minutes each day to focused planning, you can set yourself up for success, stay aligned with your broader goals, and maintain a clear sense of direction in your personal and professional life.

THREE: THE PRIORITIZATION MATRIX. A DEEPER DIVE

P rioritization is an essential skill for effective management, and using matrices and frameworks can greatly enhance your ability to make informed decisions. One of the most popular tools for prioritization is the Eisenhower Matrix, which divides tasks into four categories based on urgency and importance. This matrix helps you focus on high-priority tasks while avoiding distractions from less critical activities. By regularly categorizing your tasks within this framework, you can ensure that your time and energy are directed toward achieving your most important goals.

Another powerful prioritization tool is the ABCDE Method,[5] which categorizes tasks by their impact on your goals. Tasks labeled "A" are the most important and have significant consequences if not completed. "B" tasks are important but less critical, while "C" tasks are those that would be nice to do but have minimal impact. "D" tasks should be delegated, and "E" tasks should be eliminated. This method forces you to critically evaluate the importance of each task and prioritize accordingly, ensuring that your efforts are aligned with your objectives.

The Pareto Principle,[6] also known as the 80/20 Rule, is another effective framework for prioritization. This principle states that 80% of results come from 20% of efforts. By identifying and focusing on the tasks that contribute the most to your goals, you can maximize productivity and efficiency. This approach requires regular review and analysis of your tasks and outcomes to identify the key activities that drive many of your results.

Kanban[7] boards, popularized by the agile methodology, provide a visual framework for prioritization and task management. By organizing tasks into columns such as "To Do," "In Progress," and "Done," you can visualize your workflow and prioritize tasks based on their current status. This method is particularly effective for team-based projects, as it promotes transparency and collaboration. Kanban boards help you identify bottlenecks and prioritize tasks that move the project forward.

The RICE Scoring Model[8] is a quantitative framework used to prioritize tasks based on four factors: Reach, Impact, Confidence, and Effort. By assigning scores to each task in these categories, you can calculate a RICE score that helps you prioritize tasks objectively. This model is particularly useful for product management and development, where multiple factors must be considered when prioritizing features and initiatives. By using the RICE model, you can make data-driven decisions and ensure that your resources are allocated to the most impactful tasks.

My goal for sharing these prioritization frameworks is to provide examples of how to organize your thinking around this topic. Finding the right approach will be up to you.

How To Handle Competing Priorities And Urgent Tasks

Handling competing priorities and urgent tasks is a common challenge in management. One effective strategy is to use a prioritization matrix to categorize and address these tasks systematically.

Here again the Eisenhower Matrix, for example, helps you distinguish between urgent and important tasks, enabling you to focus on what truly matters while managing immediate demands. By categorizing tasks as urgent-important, important-not urgent, urgent-not important, and neither urgent nor important, you can make informed decisions about where to direct your efforts.

When faced with multiple urgent tasks, the ABCDE Method can help you prioritize based on the impact of each task. By labeling tasks according to their significance and consequences, you can identify which urgent tasks are truly critical and which can be postponed or delegated. This approach ensures that you address the most impactful tasks first, even when dealing with competing priorities. It also helps you avoid the trap of constantly reacting to urgent but less important tasks.

Time-blocking, as mentioned previously, is another effective technique for managing competing priorities. By allocating specific time slots for high-priority tasks and urgent activities, you can create a structured schedule that ensures important tasks receive the attention they deserve. This method helps you maintain focus and productivity, even when juggling multiple priorities. Additionally, time-blocking can include buffer periods to handle unexpected urgent tasks, allowing you to stay flexible and responsive without compromising your overall plan.

Delegation is a crucial skill for managing competing priorities. When faced with an overwhelming number of tasks, identifying which tasks can be delegated to team members can help you focus on high-priority activities. Effective delegation involves clearly communicating expectations, providing the necessary resources and support, and trusting your team to handle the tasks. By delegating appropriately, you can free up your time for strategic decision-making and high-impact activities.

The 2-Minute Rule,[9] popularized by productivity expert David Allen, is a simple yet powerful strategy for managing urgent tasks. The rule states that if a task can be completed in two minutes or less, it should be done immediately. This approach helps you quickly address small but urgent tasks, preventing them from accumulating and becoming overwhelming. By incorporating the 2-Minute Rule into your workflow, you can maintain momentum and reduce the cognitive load of managing multiple priorities.

Another strategy is to use the MoSCoW Method[10] (Must, Should, Could, Won't) for prioritizing tasks.

This method helps you categorize tasks based on their necessity and impact. "Must" tasks are critical and must be completed, "Should" tasks are important but not essential, "Could" tasks are desirable but not necessary, and "Won't" tasks are those that can be deferred or eliminated. By applying the MoSCoW Method, you can systematically address competing priorities and ensure that critical tasks are completed first.

Finally, maintaining extreme focus is essential for handling competing priorities and urgent tasks. This involves eliminating distractions, setting clear boundaries, and committing to focused work periods. Techniques such as the Pomodoro Technique, where you work in focused intervals with short breaks, can help you maintain concentration and productivity. By adopting strategies for extreme focus, you can effectively manage competing priorities, stay on top of urgent tasks, and achieve your goals efficiently.

FOUR: DELEGATION MASTERY. NOT ME, NOT NOW IN ACTION

Mastering delegation is a critical skill for effective management, and advanced delegation techniques can help you distribute tasks more efficiently while empowering your team. One such technique as described in Michael Hyatt's book, "Free to Focus" is the "5 Levels of Delegation" model, which provides a structured approach to delegating tasks based on the level of autonomy you wish to grant. The levels range from "Level 1: Do as I say," where you give explicit instructions, to "Level 5: You decide," where the team member has full autonomy to make decisions. By using this model, you can tailor your delegation approach to the capabilities and confidence of each team member, ensuring tasks are completed effectively.

Another advanced technique is the "Delegation Triangle," which is often credited to Ken Blanchard and emphasizes the importance of responsibility, authority, and accountability. The three points of the triangle are used to build trust and empower your team members. By focusing on these elements, you can create a strong foundation for successful delegation. Clear instructions, regular check-ins, and providing necessary resources are essential components of this technique, ensuring that delegated tasks are understood and executed efficiently.

The "Situational Leadership" model as presented by Paul Hersey and Ken Blanchard is also valuable for advanced delegation. This model suggests that the level of guidance and support you provide should vary depending on the team's maturity and competence. For inexperienced team members, a more directive approach may be necessary, while experienced members may require only support and encouragement. By adapting your leadership style to the needs of your team, you can enhance their performance and confidence, making delegation more effective and empowering.

Using the "SMART Criteria"[12] (Specific, Measurable, Achievable, Relevant, Time-bound) originally introduced by George T. Doran for practical goal setting is also useful for delegating tasks to ensure that objectives are clear and attainable. When delegating, it is important to define tasks using these criteria to provide clear direction and set realistic expectations. This approach not only helps team members understand what is expected of them but also allows for better tracking of progress and outcomes. By setting SMART goals, you can enhance accountability and ensure that delegated tasks contribute meaningfully to overall objectives.

The "Feedforward"[12] technique is a proactive approach to delegation, focusing on providing constructive feedback before tasks are completed rather than after. This technique involves discussing potential challenges and offering guidance on how to overcome them during the delegation process. By anticipating issues and providing support upfront, you can increase the likelihood of successful task completion. Feedforward is particularly useful for complex or critical tasks, where early intervention can prevent mistakes and improve outcomes.

Empowering Your Team To Take

Ownership

Empowering your team to take ownership of their tasks and responsibilities is essential for fostering a culture of accountability and high performance. One effective way to achieve this is by involving team members in decision-making processes. When team members have a say in how tasks are approached and executed, they are more likely to feel invested in the outcomes. This sense of ownership can lead to increased motivation, creativity, and commitment to achieving goals.

Encouraging autonomy is another key aspect of empowerment. By giving team-members the freedom to make decisions and solve problems independently, you demonstrate trust in their abilities and judgment. This approach not only boosts their confidence but also fosters a sense of responsibility. To support autonomy, it is important to provide the necessary resources, training, and support, ensuring that team members have everything they need to succeed.

Setting clear expectations and providing regular feedback are crucial for empowering your team. Clearly defined roles, responsibilities, and performance standards help team members understand what is expected of them. Regular feedback, both positive and constructive, helps them stay on track and continuously improve. Recognizing and celebrating achievements also reinforces a sense of ownership and motivates team members to maintain high performance.

Encouraging continuous learning and development is another way to empower your team. Providing opportunities for professional growth, such as training programs, workshops, and mentorship, helps team members build new skills and gain confidence. When team members see that their growth is valued, they are more likely to take initiative and strive for excellence. Supporting their development also prepares them to take on more complex tasks and responsibilities in the future.

Creating a supportive and collaborative team environment is essential for fostering ownership. When team members feel supported by their peers and managers, they are more likely to take risks, share ideas, and take responsibility for their work. Promoting open communication, mutual respect, and teamwork helps build a positive work culture where everyone feels valued and empowered. By fostering a sense of community and collaboration, you can enhance the overall performance and satisfaction of your team.

Using technology to facilitate delegation and

empowerment can also be highly effective. Tools such as project management software, communication platforms, and collaborative apps can streamline task assignment, tracking, and feedback. These tools provide transparency, enable efficient communication, and allow team members to monitor their progress and take ownership of their tasks. By leveraging technology, you can create a more organized and empowering work environment.

Promoting a growth mindset within your team encourages members to embrace challenges and view failures as learning opportunities. By fostering a culture where mistakes are seen as part of the growth process, you can reduce fear of failure and encourage experimentation and innovation. Supporting a growth mindset involves providing constructive feedback, encouraging reflection, and celebrating improvements and successes. This approach helps team members develop resilience and a proactive attitude towards their work.

Finally, leading by example is one of the most powerful ways to empower your team. Demonstrating a strong work ethic, accountability, and commitment to continuous improvement sets a standard for your team to follow. When team members see their leader taking ownership of their responsibilities and actively contributing to the team's success, they are more likely to emulate these behaviors. By modeling the qualities you wish to see in your team, you can inspire and motivate them to take ownership and excel in their roles.

FIVE: PROACTIVE LEADERSHIP. ANTICIPATING CHALLENGES

Proactive leadership involves not only reacting to problems as they arise but also anticipating challenges before they occur. One effective technique for anticipating potential issues is conducting regular risk assessments. This involves identifying possible risks in your projects or operations, assessing their likelihood and potential impact, and developing mitigation strategies. By systematically evaluating potential problems, you can prepare for them in advance, reducing their impact on your work.

Another technique is scenario planning, which involves creating detailed plans for various future scenarios. This method allows you to explore different outcomes and develop strategies for dealing with each one. Scenario planning helps you think critically about potential challenges and devise flexible responses. This approach can be particularly useful in uncertain environments, where being prepared for a range of possibilities can provide a significant advantage.

Maintaining open lines of communication with your team is crucial for anticipating challenges. Regular check-ins and feedback sessions can help you stay informed about potential issues and emerging concerns. Encouraging team members to voice their thoughts and observations can provide valuable insights into potential problems that may not be immediately apparent. This proactive communication helps you address issues early and develop solutions collaboratively.

Using data analytics and monitoring tools can also help you anticipate and mitigate potential issues. By tracking key performance indicators and analyzing trends, you can identify warning signs of potential problems before they escalate. For example, monitoring project timelines, resource utilization, and team performance can help you spot bottlenecks and take corrective action. Leveraging technology in this way enhances your ability to stay ahead of challenges and make informed decisions.

Developing contingency plans is another essential aspect of proactive leadership. These plans outline specific actions to take in response to various potential issues, ensuring that you and your team are prepared to act quickly and effectively. Contingency plans should be regularly reviewed and updated to reflect changing circumstances and new information. Having these plans in place provides a sense of security and readiness, allowing you to navigate challenges with confidence.

Building Resilience In Your Team

Building resilience in your team is crucial for navigating challenges and maintaining high performance under pressure. One effective way to foster resilience is by promoting a growth mindset. Encouraging team members to view challenges as opportunities for learning and growth helps them develop a more positive and proactive attitude. This mindset shift can reduce fear of failure and increase their willingness to take on difficult tasks and innovate.

Providing ongoing training and development opportunities is another key strategy for building resilience. By equipping your team with the skills and knowledge they need to handle challenges, you increase their confidence and ability to adapt. This includes both technical skills and soft skills such as problem-solving, communication, and stress management. Continuous learning helps team members stay flexible and capable in the face of changing demands.

Creating a supportive team culture is essential for fostering resilience. When team members feel supported by their peers and leaders, they are more likely to persevere through difficult times. Promoting open communication, mutual respect, and collaboration helps build a strong sense of community and belonging. Encouraging team bonding activities and providing emotional support can also strengthen the team's resilience and cohesiveness.

Encouraging autonomy and empowerment within your team can enhance their resilience. When team members have the freedom to make decisions and take ownership of their work, they develop a greater sense of responsibility and confidence. This autonomy fosters problem-solving skills and creativity, enabling them to handle challenges more effectively. Supporting their decisions and providing the necessary resources further reinforces their ability to navigate difficulties.

Recognizing and celebrating successes, both big and small, can boost team morale and resilience. Acknowledging the efforts and achievements of your team members helps build their confidence and motivation. Regularly highlighting successes creates a positive environment where team members feel valued and appreciated. This positive reinforcement can increase their resilience and drive to overcome future challenges.

Encouraging a healthy work-life balance is also crucial for building resilience. Overworking can lead to burnout, reducing the team's ability to cope with stress and challenges. Promoting regular breaks, flexible work arrangements, and emphasizing the importance of rest and recovery can help maintain their well-being. A balanced approach to work and life enhances overall resilience and productivity.

Implementing stress management techniques and providing resources for mental health can further support resilience. Offering workshops on mindfulness, meditation, and stress reduction can equip team members with tools to manage their stress effectively. Providing access to mental health resources and creating an open dialogue about mental well-being helps reduce stigma and ensures that team members feel supported.

Leading by example is one of the most powerful ways to build resilience in your team. Demonstrating resilience in your own actions, such as maintaining a positive attitude, handling stress effectively, and showing adaptability, sets a standard for your team to follow. Your behavior can inspire and motivate team members to adopt similar resilience strategies, creating a more robust and capable team overall.

It has become clear to me that fostering a culture of continuous improvement can enhance team resilience. Encouraging regular reflection and feedback helps identify areas for growth and development. This focus on continuous improvement ensures that the team is always evolving and adapting to new challenges. By promoting a culture of learning and development, you can build a resilient team that thrives in the face of adversity.

SIX: TAILORING MANAGEMENT STYLES. ONE SIZE DOESN'T FIT ALL

A laissez-faire management style, which emphasizes minimal interference and maximum autonomy for team members, can be highly effective in certain situations. For instance, when working with highly skilled and experienced team members who thrive on independence, a laissez-faire approach can empower them to take ownership of their projects and innovate freely. In creative industries, where employees often require the freedom to explore new ideas, this style can lead to significant breakthroughs and high job satisfaction.

However, it's crucial to recognize that different

team members and situations may require a shift in management style. For example, new or less experienced employees might benefit more from a coaching or directive approach. Providing clear instructions, regular feedback, and close supervision can help them build confidence and competence. As these employees develop their skills, gradually transitioning to a more autonomous style can encourage growth and independence.

Situational Leadership Theory[11,] developed by Paul Hersey and Ken Blanchard, suggests that effective leaders adjust their style based on the maturity and competence of their team members. For instance, when dealing with a high-stakes project or tight deadline, even highly competent teams may need more guidance and support. In such scenarios, a more directive approach can ensure clarity and focus, helping the team meet critical objectives efficiently.

Conversely, in routine or low-stress situations, a supportive or participative style might be more appropriate. Encouraging team members to share their ideas and participate in decision-making fosters a sense of inclusion and empowerment. This approach can be particularly effective in team-building activities or brainstorming sessions, where collective input and collaboration are essential for success.

Practical examples of adapting your style can include shifting from laissez-faire to a more supportive role when team members are facing personal challenges or high stress. Offering additional resources, being available for one-on-one check-ins, and providing emotional support can help them navigate difficult periods while maintaining productivity. Similarly, adopting a more hands-on approach during critical phases of a project can ensure that everyone stays aligned and on track.

Balancing Flexibility And Consistency

Balancing flexibility and consistency is key to effective management. While it's important to adapt your style to different situations and team members, maintaining a consistent framework for expectations and accountability is essential. Consistency in your core values, communication practices, and performance standards creates a stable environment where team members understand what is expected of them, regardless of the management style applied.

For example, maintaining regular team meetings

and performance reviews can provide a consistent touchpoint for feedback and alignment. Even within a laissez-faire framework, setting clear goals and deadlines ensures that team members remain focused and accountable. This consistency in structure allows flexibility in day-to-day management while ensuring that overall objectives are met.

A practical way to balance flexibility and consistency is through setting up a system of check-ins and milestones. For instance, while allowing team members the freedom to approach their tasks independently, scheduling regular progress reviews can help monitor their progress and provide support when needed. This approach maintains the autonomy inherent in a laissez-faire style while ensuring that projects stay on track.

Additionally, developing clear policies and procedures can provide a consistent foundation that supports flexible management. When team members know the protocols for communication, conflict resolution, and task management, they can operate more autonomously within those guidelines. This structure allows managers to adapt their style as needed without creating confusion or inconsistency in the team's operations.

Incorporating flexibility into your management

style also means being open to feedback and willing to adjust your approach based on team input. Encouraging an open dialogue where team members can express their needs and preferences allows you to tailor your management style more effectively. This practice not only enhances team satisfaction but also fosters a culture of mutual respect and collaboration.

For instance, a team member might express a need for more guidance on a particular project. In response, you could temporarily adopt a more directive style, providing detailed instructions and regular feedback until they feel confident to proceed independently. Conversely, if a team member demonstrates a high level of competence and initiative, you might increase their autonomy, supporting them in taking on more responsibility and leadership within the team.

Balancing flexibility and consistency also involve being mindful of the team's overall dynamics. For example, during periods of change or uncertainty, such as organizational restructuring or market shifts, maintaining a consistent approach to communication and support can provide stability and reassurance. At the same time, being flexible in adapting strategies and roles to navigate the new landscape effectively demonstrates your responsiveness and resilience as a leader.

Ultimately, tailoring your management style to fit different team members and situations while maintaining a balance between flexibility and consistency can lead to a more dynamic and productive work environment. By understanding the unique needs of your team and adapting your approach accordingly, you can foster a culture of empowerment, innovation, and continuous improvement. This balanced approach ensures that your team can thrive in various contexts, driving success and achieving collective goals.

SEVEN: VIRTUAL LEADERSHIP. A NEW REALITY.

The global pandemic has significantly accelerated the shift to remote and hybrid work models, forcing organizations and leaders to adapt to a new reality. Leading remote and hybrid teams effectively requires a different set of skills and practices compared to traditional in-person management. One of the most crucial aspects is establishing clear communication channels. Regular video meetings, consistent use of messaging platforms, and clear email protocols help ensure that everyone stays informed and connected, despite physical distances.

I have been fortunate to work in an industry where working remotely is the norm and showing up at an office isn't expected. So, making this adjustment was a little different in that regular travel to customer meetings, conferences, and other events was severely limited. We had to come up with creative ways to drive the needed interaction with prospective customers and team members. In addition to video meetings, we found incorporating collaboration tools highly effective tools to engage in more substantive activities.

One of the lessons learned during this time was that even well-intentioned people will experience times of low productivity and low engagement. It also became clear that the shift in remote work created a culture where many no longer want to be bound by traditional work structures making it difficult to find and retain staff. This is where good leadership can make all the difference.

Setting clear expectations and goals is another critical practice for virtual leadership. When team members work remotely, they need to understand what is expected of them in terms of deliverables, deadlines, and work hours. This clarity helps prevent misunderstandings and ensures that everyone is aligned with the team's objectives. Additionally, providing regular feedback and performance reviews helps maintain accountability and continuous improvement.

Building trust within remote and hybrid teams

is essential for fostering a positive and productive work environment. Trust can be cultivated by promoting transparency, being available for one-on-one check-ins, and showing empathy toward team members' challenges and needs. When team members feel trusted and supported, they are more likely to take initiative and perform at their best. Encouraging a culture of mutual respect and understanding also helps strengthen team cohesion.

Maintaining team cohesion and morale can be challenging in a remote setting, but it is not impossible. Virtual team-building activities, such as online games, virtual coffee breaks, and team challenges, can help create a sense of camaraderie and connection. Celebrating milestones and recognizing individual and team achievements through virtual channels also helps boost morale and reinforce a sense of belonging.

Flexibility and adaptability are key traits for leaders managing remote and hybrid teams. Understanding that team members may face different challenges, such as varying time zones, home distractions, and differing work styles, is crucial. Offering flexible work schedules and being accommodating to individual circumstances helps create a supportive environment where team members can thrive. This approach also demonstrates empathy and respect for their well-being.

Tools And Strategies For Maintaining Engagement And Productivity

Leveraging the right tools and technologies is essential for maintaining engagement and productivity in remote and hybrid teams. Project management software such as Jira, and Trello, mentioned earlier, helps teams organize tasks, track progress, and collaborate effectively. These platforms provide a centralized space where team members can see what needs to be done, who is responsible, and the status of each task, ensuring transparency and accountability.

Communication tools like Slack, Microsoft Teams, or Zoom are vital for facilitating real-time interactions and keeping team members connected. These tools offer various features, such as chat channels, video conferencing, file sharing, and integrations with other software, making it easier to collaborate and communicate efficiently. Regular video meetings, whether for team updates, brainstorming sessions, or casual check-ins, help maintain a sense of connection and engagement.

To keep team members engaged, it's important to foster a sense of community and belonging. Virtual social events, such as online happy hours, trivia nights, or book clubs, provide opportunities for team members to connect on a personal level and build relationships. Encouraging informal interactions through dedicated chat channels for non-work-related topics also helps create a more cohesive and engaged team.

Performance tracking and productivity tools like Time Doctor[p8], Toggl[p9], or RescueTime[p10] can help remote teams stay focused and efficient. These tools provide insights into how time is spent, helping team members identify areas for improvement and optimize their work habits. For leaders, these tools offer visibility into team productivity and can inform decisions on workload distribution and resource allocation. I have used time and productivity tracking tools in the past, they have their place. However, if you're in a business where more focus is on the outcomes and less on the activities of the employee, then you can likely avoid using these tools. Creating a culture of ownership and accountability will go a long way toward setting and managing individual contributions to your business.

Encouraging continuous learning and

professional development is another strategy for maintaining engagement and productivity. Offering access to online courses, webinars, and training programs helps team members enhance their skills and stay motivated. Creating a culture of learning and growth not only benefits individual team members but also strengthens the overall capability and resilience of the team.

Implementing regular check-ins and feedback loops is crucial for staying connected with remote and hybrid teams. Weekly or bi-weekly one-on-one meetings provide opportunities to discuss progress, address concerns, and offer support. These check-ins help leaders stay attuned to their team members' needs and foster a sense of accountability and engagement. Additionally, soliciting feedback from team members on what is working well and where improvements can be made helps create a more responsive and adaptive work environment.

Balancing work and personal life can be challenging in a remote setting, so promoting a healthy work-life balance is essential. Encouraging team members to set boundaries, take regular breaks, and disconnect after work hours helps prevent burnout and maintain overall well-being. Leaders can model this behavior by respecting boundaries and not expecting immediate responses outside of designated work hours.

Recognizing and celebrating achievements is vital for maintaining morale and motivation in remote and hybrid teams. Whether through virtual shout-outs, digital badges, or formal recognition programs, acknowledging individual and team accomplishments reinforces a culture of appreciation and support. Celebrating successes, both big and small, helps build a positive and motivated team environment.

Lastly, embracing flexibility and adaptability in your leadership approach is key to managing remote and hybrid teams effectively. Being open to new ideas, experimenting with different tools and strategies, and continuously seeking ways to improve the remote work experience demonstrates a commitment to your team's success. By staying agile and responsive to the evolving needs of your team, you can create a thriving remote and hybrid work environment that drives engagement and productivity.

EIGHT: COACHING VS. MENTORING VS. MANAGING. APPLIED TECHNIQUES

Understanding the distinct roles of coaching, mentoring, and managing is essential for effective leadership. Each approach serves a different purpose and can be used to achieve specific outcomes based on the needs of your team members and the situation at hand. Managing typically involves overseeing day-to-day operations, setting goals, and ensuring tasks are completed efficiently. Managers focus on maintaining productivity, meeting deadlines, and aligning team efforts with organizational objectives. This approach is crucial when clear guidance, structure, and accountability are needed.

Coaching, on the other hand, emphasizes developing individual skills and performance through feedback and guidance. Coaches work closely with team members to identify strengths and areas for improvement, set personal development goals, and provide ongoing support. Coaching is particularly effective when a team member needs to enhance specific skills, overcome challenges, or achieve short-term performance targets. It is a collaborative process that encourages self-reflection and growth.

Mentoring involves a longer-term relationship focused on personal and professional development. Mentors provide wisdom, advice, and support based on their own experiences, helping mentees navigate their career paths and make informed decisions. This approach is valuable when team members seek guidance on broader career goals, professional growth, and navigating organizational culture. Mentors serve as role models and trusted advisors, offering insights and encouragement.

Choosing the right approach depends on the individual needs and context. For instance, if a team member is struggling with a specific task or needs to develop a particular skill, coaching is the appropriate choice. If they are seeking broader career advice or looking to develop long-term professional relationships, mentoring is more suitable. When the focus is on achieving immediate organizational goals and ensuring team performance, managing is the primary approach.

Real-Life Examples And Success Stories

Consider this case, as a professional services leader at a business technology consulting company, I noticed that one of my team members, Ray, had strong analytical skills but struggled with presenting his idea confidently in client meetings. Recognizing this, I decided to take a coaching approach. I worked with Ray to improve his presentation skills, producing constructive feedback and setting specific goals. Over time, Ray's confidence grew, and he became an effective communicator, a master at presenting complex concepts in a simplified way and contributing more significantly to team discussions and projects.

In another example, at a software manufacturer, as a senior technical executive, I took on the role of mentor for a promising young employee, Bernard. I shared my experiences, offered career advice, and introduced Bernard to the value of professional networks. This mentoring relationship helped Bernard gain clarity on his career goals and develop a strategic approach to his professional development. With guidance, Bernard successfully navigated several career transitions and achieved his career objectives.

Managing effectively can be seen in the example of a project management role. I led a team through a critical program launch. I established clear goals, set deadlines, and monitored progress closely. I held regular team meetings to ensure alignment and address any issues promptly. Maintaining a structured and goal-oriented approach helped to ensure that the project was completed on time and met all quality standards, showcasing the importance of strong management in achieving organizational success.

Finally, consider another success story that involves a hybrid approach. As a first-line manager of a technical sales team, I used a combination of coaching, mentoring, and management to support a diverse team. I provided coaching to develop specific skills, mentored team members seeking career advancement and managed the overall team performance to meet departmental goals. By tailoring my approach to individual needs, I created a cohesive and high-performing team.

In each of these examples, my goal is to highlight that it's important to adjust your approach to fit the specific needs of your team members and the context, demonstrating the effectiveness of coaching, mentoring, and managing when applied appropriately. By understanding and utilizing these different techniques, leaders can support their teams' growth, performance, and overall success.

NINE: SUSTAINABILITY IN MANAGEMENT. LONG-TERM SUCCESS

Sustainable management practices are essential for achieving long-term success in any organization. One effective strategy is to implement a strong foundation of ethical principles and social responsibility. In my experience teams rooted in shared values promises to maintain consistent management practices. By prioritizing ethical behavior and making socially responsible decisions, organizations can build trust with stakeholders, including employees, customers, and the broader community. This trust is crucial for maintaining a positive reputation and ensuring long-term sustainability. I have found that if you treat people like adult professionals, they feel respected and respond more favorability when encountering difficult situations.

Another key strategy is to foster a culture of continuous improvement. Encouraging employees to regularly assess and enhance their skills and processes helps keep the organization agile and responsive to changes. Continuous improvement can be driven through regular training programs, feedback loops, and performance reviews, ensuring that everyone in the organization is aligned with the goal of sustained progress and innovation.

Effective resource management is crucial for minimizing wasted time and underutilized talent. In addition to focusing on material or energy utilization, organizations must prioritize optimizing human resources to maximize productivity and avoid inefficiencies. Wasting time or failing to leverage employees' skills not only hinders overall performance but also reduces organizational potential. By strategically managing people and their contributions, organizations can enhance long-term success, fostering a more efficient and sustainable work environment where human potential is fully realized. A useful exercise to periodically evaluate that your team is focused on business priorities is to ask, "What can we stop doing and use that time for what's important?" You'll be surprised how much of your team's time is spent on doing things that are not or no longer required for managing the business.

Employee well-being and engagement are critical to long-term success. Investing in the health, safety, and professional development of employees fosters a motivated and loyal workforce. Providing benefits such as health insurance, mental health support, flexible working arrangements, and opportunities for career advancement can enhance employee satisfaction and retention. A healthy and engaged workforce is more productive and better equipped to contribute to the organization's long-term goals.

Transparency and accountability are essential for sustainable management. Regularly communicating the organization's goals, challenges, and achievements helps build trust and ensure that everyone is on the same page. Implementing robust governance structures and accountability mechanisms ensures that decisions are made responsibly and align with the long-term vision. Transparent practices also facilitate stakeholder engagement and support.

Balancing Short-Term Goals With Long-Term Vision

Balancing short-term goals with a long-term vision requires a strategic approach to planning and decision-making. One effective method is to set clear, measurable objectives that align with the organization's long-term vision. These objectives should be broken down into short-term milestones that can be achieved incrementally. This approach allows for progress tracking and adjustments while keeping the organization focused on its long-term goals.

Scenario planning is another valuable tool for balancing short-term and long-term priorities. By anticipating various future scenarios and developing corresponding strategies, organizations can prepare for potential challenges and opportunities. Scenario planning helps ensure that short-term actions are informed by long-term considerations, enabling more resilient and adaptable decision-making.

Effective time management is crucial for balancing immediate needs with future aspirations. Prioritizing tasks and projects based on their alignment with both short-term objectives and long-term vision helps ensure that urgent matters do not overshadow important strategic initiatives. Time management tools and techniques, such as the Eisenhower Matrix, can help leaders make informed decisions about where to allocate their efforts and resources.

Regularly reviewing and adjusting the strategic plan is essential for maintaining balance. This involves assessing progress towards short-term goals and making necessary adjustments to stay on track for long-term success. Flexibility and adaptability are key, as changing circumstances may require shifts in strategy. Regular reviews ensure that the organization remains aligned with its long-term vision while responding effectively to short-term challenges.

Innovation plays a critical role in achieving long-term sustainability. Encouraging a culture of innovation helps organizations stay competitive and adapt to changing market conditions. This can be achieved by investing in research and development, fostering creative thinking, and supporting initiatives that drive technological advancements and process improvements. By prioritizing innovation, organizations can build a foundation for sustained growth and success.

Stakeholder engagement is another important aspect of balancing short-term and long-term goals. Engaging with stakeholders, including employees, customers, investors, and the community, provides valuable insights into their needs and expectations. This engagement helps ensure that the organization's short-term actions are aligned with stakeholder interests and contribute to long-term success. Building strong relationships with stakeholders also enhances trust and support for the organization's vision.

Maintaining financial health is essential for long-term sustainability. This involves prudent financial management, including budgeting, cost control, and investment in growth opportunities. Diversifying revenue streams and building financial reserves can help organizations navigate economic uncertainties and invest in long-term initiatives. Sound financial practices ensure that the organization can achieve its short-term goals while building a stable foundation for the future.

Leadership development is crucial for sustaining long-term success. Investing in the development of current and future leaders ensures that the organization has the talent and skills needed to navigate challenges and seize opportunities. Leadership development programs, mentorship, and succession planning help build a pipeline of capable leaders who can drive the organization's long-term vision.

Technology adoption is a key driver of long-term success. Embracing new technologies can enhance productivity, streamline operations, and open new business opportunities. Investing in digital transformation, automation, and data analytics helps organizations stay competitive and responsive to market changes. Technology adoption should be aligned with the organization's long-term vision to ensure that investments support strategic goals.

Corporate governance is fundamental to balancing short-term actions with long-term vision. Strong governance structures and practices ensure that the organization operates with integrity, transparency, and accountability. This includes establishing clear policies, oversight mechanisms, and ethical standards that guide decision-making. Good governance builds stakeholder trust and supports sustainable growth.

Building a resilient organization is essential for long-term success. Resilience involves the ability to adapt to disruptions, recover from setbacks, and continue progressing toward strategic goals. This can be achieved through robust risk management practices, diversification of products and services, and fostering a culture of agility and innovation. Resilience ensures that the organization can withstand challenges and capitalize on opportunities over the long term.

Fostering a culture of sustainability within the

organization is key to achieving long-term success. This involves embedding sustainability principles into the organization's values, policies, and everyday practices. Encouraging sustainable behaviors, recognizing contributions to sustainability, and integrating sustainability into decision-making processes help create a culture where long-term success is a shared priority. By making sustainability a core part of the organizational culture, leaders can ensure that the pursuit of long-term goals is embraced by everyone in the organization.

TEN: NETWORKING AND INFLUENCE. YOUR PROFESSIONAL BRAND

Building a strong professional network is crucial for career advancement and personal development. Advanced networking strategies go beyond simply making connections; they focus on creating meaningful relationships that can provide mutual support and opportunities. One effective strategy is to approach networking with a giver's mindset. By offering help, resources, or introductions to others without expecting immediate returns, you build goodwill and a reputation as a valuable and generous connection.

Another advanced strategy is to be strategic about where and how you network. This involves identifying key industry events, conferences, and seminars where influential professionals gather.

Attending these events allows you to meet thought leaders, potential mentors, and peers who can provide insights and opportunities. Being selective about the events you attend ensures that your networking efforts are focused and productive.

Online networking has become increasingly important, especially in the wake of the global pandemic. Platforms like LinkedIn offer powerful tools for connecting with professionals across the globe. To leverage these platforms effectively, it's important to maintain an active and engaging profile. Regularly sharing valuable content, participating in discussions, and endorsing others' skills can help you build a strong online presence and attract connections who share your professional interests.

Joining professional organizations and associations related to your field can also enhance your networking efforts. These groups often offer exclusive events, resources, and forums for members to connect and collaborate. Being an active member and participating in these activities can help you build relationships with peers and leaders in your industry, providing valuable opportunities for learning and growth.

Mentorship programs, both formal and informal, are another powerful networking strategy. Seeking out mentors who can provide guidance and support can accelerate your career development. Similarly, offering to mentor others can expand your network and establish you as a leader in your field. These relationships often lead to deeper connections and long-term professional support.

Leveraging Your Network For Career Growth And Opportunities

Once you have built a strong network, it's important to leverage these connections effectively for career growth and opportunities. One of the most significant benefits of a robust network is access to information and insights. Your connections can provide valuable knowledge about industry trends, job openings, and best practices. Regularly engaging with your network ensures that you stay informed and ahead of the curve in your professional field.

A well-established network can also provide direct career opportunities. Many job openings are filled through referrals and personal recommendations. By maintaining strong relationships with your contacts, you increase the likelihood that you will be considered for new roles and opportunities. Networking can often lead to unadvertised positions and unique career paths that might not be accessible through traditional job search methods.

Collaborative projects and partnerships are another way to leverage your network. Working with others on joint ventures, research projects, or business initiatives can enhance your skills, expand your experience, and increase your visibility in your industry. These collaborations often lead to new opportunities and strengthen your professional brand as a collaborative and innovative leader.

Networking also plays a crucial role in personal branding. Your reputation within your network can significantly influence your career trajectory. A good reputation, built on reliability, professionalism, and integrity, can open doors to new opportunities and partnerships. By consistently demonstrating these qualities, you enhance your brand and become a sought-after professional in your field.

Engaging with thought leaders and influencers in your industry can further enhance your professional brand. Following their work, participating in their discussions, and even collaborating on projects can elevate your profile. Being associated with respected figures in your industry lends credibility to your own brand and can attract more high-quality connections.

Continuous learning and development are essential for maintaining the value of your network. Attending workshops, earning certifications, and staying updated on industry developments ensure that you remain a knowledgeable and valuable connection. Sharing your learning journey and insights with your network can position you as a thought leader and resource, further enhancing your professional brand.

Fostering a diverse professional network is pivotal for career advancement. Consider how within your company, an IT professional might collaborate with the finance team, gaining insights on budget and business justification that enrich technology planning and strategies. Similarly, when a seasoned project manager mentors a new analytics graduate, both benefit from shared knowledge, bridging experience with fresh methodologies.

Employee Resource Groups, like veterans, neurodivergent, or multicultural initiatives, weave connections across departments, fostering inclusivity and learning. Rotational programs can further broaden your perspective, moving you through human resources to customer service and linking you with a wider network.

By actively seeking these diverse connections, you not only enhance your own skill set but also contribute to a vibrant, innovative work culture.

Maintaining regular contact with your network is essential for leveraging its full potential. Regularly reaching out to check in, help, or share updates keeps your relationships strong and active. These touchpoints can also lead to unexpected opportunities and collaborations, as staying top-of-mind with your contacts increases the likelihood of being considered for new projects and roles.

Active participation in industry-specific forums, online communities, and social media groups can also enhance your networking efforts. These platforms provide opportunities to share knowledge, ask questions, and engage in meaningful discussions with other professionals. Being an active contributor to these communities can increase your visibility and establish you as a thought leader in your field.

Your network can also provide support and guidance during career transitions. Whether you are considering a new job, changing industries, or starting your own business, your connections can offer advice, introductions, and resources to help you navigate these changes successfully. Leveraging your network during these times can smooth the transition and provide a strong foundation for your next career move.

Networking can also be a potent tool for personal growth and development. Engaging with a diverse group of professionals exposes you to different perspectives, challenges your thinking, and encourages you to step out of your comfort zone. This continuous exposure to new ideas and experiences helps you grow both personally and professionally, making you a more well-rounded and adaptable leader.

Finally, building a strong network requires authenticity and genuine interest in others. Authentic connections, based on mutual respect and genuine interest, are more likely to result in meaningful and lasting relationships. By being true to yourself and showing a sincere interest in the success and well-being of your connections, you can build a network that supports your career growth and personal development in profound ways.

ELEVEN: THE EVOLVING MANAGER. ADAPTING TO CHANGE

In a fast-changing business landscape, managers must continuously evolve to stay relevant and effective. There's good news and bad news. First, some bad news, getting up to speed and staying up to speed takes a lot of time and effort. The good news? There's bound to be someone around you "who's been there and done that." With that in mind let's cover some strategies to help you evolve and adapt.

One key strategy is to embrace adaptability. This involves being open to change, actively seeking out new information, and being willing to adjust strategies and approaches as needed. Flexibility in thought and action allows managers to respond swiftly to market shifts, technological advancements, and evolving customer needs.

Staying informed about industry trends and emerging technologies is crucial for maintaining relevance. Managers should regularly engage with industry publications, attend conferences, and participate in professional networks. This ongoing engagement provides insights into new developments and best practices, enabling managers to anticipate changes and prepare their teams accordingly. Being proactive in acquiring new knowledge helps managers stay ahead of the curve.

Networking and building relationships with peers and thought leaders in the industry can provide valuable perspectives and opportunities for collaboration. These connections can offer support, advice, and shared experiences that enhance a manager's ability to navigate change. Engaging in professional communities also facilitates the exchange of ideas and strategies, contributing to continuous learning and adaptation.

Facilitating a culture of innovation within the team is another essential strategy. Encouraging team members to experiment, take risks, and propose new ideas creates an environment where innovation thrives. This culture not only leads to the development of new solutions and improvements but also helps the team become more resilient and adaptable. Managers can support this by providing resources, recognition, and a safe space for creative thinking.

Embracing technology and leveraging digital tools can significantly enhance a manager's effectiveness. From project management software to data analytics tools, technology can streamline processes, improve decision-making, and increase efficiency. Managers should stay updated on technological advancements relevant to their industry and explore how these tools can be integrated into their operations. This proactive approach to technology adoption ensures that the team remains competitive and efficient.

Continuous Learning And Self-Improvement Techniques

Commitment to continuous learning is vital for managers who want to stay effective in a changing environment. One approach is to set aside regular time for professional development. This can include reading industry books, taking online courses, or pursuing advanced degrees and certifications. Continuous learning ensures that managers keep their skills current and are equipped to handle new challenges.

Seeking feedback from peers, mentors, and team members is another powerful tool for self-improvement. Constructive feedback provides insights into areas for growth and development that may not be immediately apparent. Managers should cultivate a feedback-friendly environment where open, honest communication is encouraged. Regular feedback sessions can help identify strengths and areas for improvement, guiding personal and professional development.

Self-reflection is an important practice for continuous improvement. Taking time to reflect on successes, failures, and experiences helps managers gain deeper insights into their behavior and decisions. Reflective practices, such as journaling or meditation, can enhance self-awareness and lead to more thoughtful and informed decision-making. This introspective approach supports ongoing growth and adaptation.

Participating in training and development programs is essential for skill enhancement. Many organizations offer leadership development programs that provide training on new management techniques, technologies, and industry trends. These programs often include workshops, seminars, and hands-on activities that help managers build new competencies. Investing in these opportunities ensures that managers are well-prepared to lead in a dynamic environment.

Mentorship, both receiving and providing, plays a crucial role in continuous learning. Having a mentor can provide guidance, support, and insights from someone with more experience. Conversely, mentoring others can enhance a manager's leadership skills and reinforce their own knowledge. This reciprocal relationship fosters a culture of learning and growth within the organization.

Engaging in cross-functional projects and roles can broaden a manager's perspective and skill set. Working with different departments or taking on new responsibilities exposes managers to diverse challenges and solutions. This experience helps build a more versatile skill set and enhances the ability to manage complex and multifaceted projects. Cross-functional experience is invaluable for adapting to change and leading diverse teams.

Staying physically and mentally healthy is critical for sustained effectiveness. Regular exercise, a balanced diet, and sufficient rest contribute to overall well-being and energy levels. Mental health practices, such as mindfulness and stress management techniques, help maintain focus and resilience. A healthy manager is better equipped to handle stress, make sound decisions, and lead by example.

Developing emotional intelligence (EQ) is essential for effective leadership. EQ involves understanding and managing one's emotions and recognizing and influencing the emotions of others. High EQ helps managers navigate interpersonal relationships, build strong teams, and handle conflict constructively. Enhancing EQ through training and practice can significantly improve a manager's ability to lead effectively in a changing environment.

Embracing a growth mindset, as proposed by psychologist Carol Dweck[14], is foundational for continuous learning and improvement. A growth mindset is the belief that abilities and intelligence can be developed through dedication and hard work. Managers with a growth mindset are more likely to embrace challenges, persist in the face of setbacks, and see effort as a path to mastery. This mindset fosters resilience and a proactive approach to self-improvement.

Engaging in professional coaching can provide personalized guidance and development. Professional coaches work with managers to identify goals, overcome obstacles, and develop strategies for improvement. This targeted support helps managers refine their skills, enhance performance, and achieve their full potential. Coaching can be particularly beneficial during times of significant change or transition.

Maintaining a balanced approach to work and personal life is crucial for long-term success. Ensuring that there is time for relaxation, hobbies, friends, and family helps prevent burnout and maintain motivation. Work-life balance contributes to overall happiness and productivity, enabling managers to bring their best selves to their professional roles. By prioritizing balance, managers can sustain their effectiveness and well-being over the long term.

EMBRACING THE JOURNEY OF LEADERSHIP

As we bring this book to a close, it's important to reflect on the journey you've undertaken to enhance your management skills and leadership abilities. The concepts and strategies you've explored are more than just tools—they are the foundation for becoming a leader who not only meets challenges but thrives in them. Leadership is an ongoing journey, and the knowledge you've gained here is meant to be a companion on that path, guiding you as you navigate the complexities of managing people, projects, and your own growth.

Throughout this book, we've delved into advanced organizational strategies, efficient planning techniques, and the art of prioritization.

These are not just about getting more done, but about getting the right things done. It's about clarity of purpose and precision in action. As you apply these techniques, remember that true productivity is not measured by the length of your to-do list but by the impact of your actions. Focus on what truly matters and let that guide your daily decisions.

We also explored the importance of empowering your team through delegation and tailored management styles. The best leaders know that their success is intertwined with the success of their team. By giving your team the tools, guidance, and autonomy they need, you not only lighten your own load but also build a stronger, more resilient organization. Trust in your team's abilities, and they will rise to meet—and often exceed—your expectations.

Leadership today demands more than just responding to what's in front of you; it requires anticipation and preparation. Being proactive, anticipating challenges, and adapting to change are essential skills for any leader who wants to stay relevant and effective. The world is constantly evolving, and those who succeed are the ones who embrace change, learn continuously, and remain flexible in their approach. Keep your mind open, stay curious, and never stop learning.

In the increasingly digital and remote world we live in, mastering virtual leadership has become a critical skill. Leading from afar requires a different kind of presence—one that is felt through consistent communication, trust-building, and maintaining a strong team culture, even when the team is dispersed. Whether your team is in the same building or spread across the globe, your ability to connect, engage, and inspire remains your most powerful tool.

As you continue to grow in your leadership role, remember the balance between short-term objectives and long-term vision. Sustainable success is not about quick wins but about building something that lasts. It's about making decisions today that will benefit you, your team, and your organization tomorrow and beyond. Stay true to your values, keep your goals in sight, and lead with the future in mind.

Networking and personal branding have never been more important. The relationships you build and the reputation you cultivate are integral to your success as a leader. Approach networking not as a transaction but as a genuine opportunity to connect, learn, and grow with others. Your professional brand is built on trust, integrity, and the value you bring to your network—nurture it with care and intention.

In closing, I want to remind you that leadership is a journey, not a destination. There will always be new challenges to face, new skills to learn, and new heights to reach. But with the strategies and insights you've gained from this book, you are well-equipped to navigate that journey with confidence and purpose. Keep pushing yourself, keep refining your approach, and most importantly, keep believing in your ability to lead and inspire those around you.

Your journey as a leader is uniquely yours, and it will evolve with every experience, every success, and every setback. Embrace it fully and remember that the greatest leaders are those who never stop learning, growing, and striving to be better. Here's to your continued success—may your leadership journey be as rewarding as it is impactful.

REFERENCES & RESOURCES

Articles

1 Introducing the Eisenhower Matrix. https://www.eisenhower.me/eisenhower-matrix/
Eisenhower Matrix: Nevins, Mark. (2023). How To Get Stuff Done: The Eisenhower Matrix (a.k.a. The Urgent Vs The Important). https://www.forbes.com/sites/hillennevins/2023/01/05/how-to-get-stuff-done-the-eisenhower-matrix-aka-the-urgent-vs-the-important/

2 Richardson, Ric. (2023). The Real Reason Elon Musk Does 5-Minute Scheduling. https://www.linkedin.com/pulse/real-reason-elon-musk-does-5-minute-scheduling-ric-richardson-yeemc/

3 Dutta, Swarnali. (2023). 5-Minute time blocking: Secret sauce to Elon Musk's success. https://yourstory.com/2023/11/elon-musk-5-minute-rule-increases-productivity

4 Everett, Robert. (2024). IBM Design Thinking

Model explained. https://www.toolshero.com/
creativity/ibm-design-thinking/

5 ABCDE Method: Tracy, Brian. (2017). How To Set
Priorities Using The ABCDE Method. https://
www.briantracy.com/blog/time-management/the-
abcde-list-technique-for-setting-priorities/

6 Pareto Principle (80/20 Rule): Olivia Guy-Evans, MSc
(2023). Pareto Principle (The 80-20 Rule): Examples
& More. https://www.simplypsychology.org/
pareto-principle.html

7 Kanban: Halton, Clay (2024). What Is the Kanban
System? https://www.investopedia.com/terms/
k/kanban.asp

8 RICE Scoring Model: Kao, Clement. (2022). What is
the RICE Scoring Model for Prioritization? https://
www.productteacher.com/articles/product-
manager-guide-to-rice-prioritization

9 2-Minute Rule: Groenewegen, Carla (2024).
How to Use the 2-Minute Rule for More
Productivity and Less Procrastination. https://
www.usemotion.com/blog/2-minute-rule

10 MoSCoW Method: Wikipedia. (2024). MoSCoW
method. https://en.wikipedia.org/wiki/
MoSCoW_method

11 Situational Leadership: Wikipedia.
(2024). Situational Leadership theory.
https://en.wikipedia.org/wiki/
Situational_leadership_theory

12 SMART Criteria (1): Doran, George T.
(1981). There's a S.M.A.R.T. way to write
management's goals and objectives.

https://community.mis.temple.edu/
mis0855002fall2015/files/2015/10/S.M.A.R.T-
Way-Management-Review.pdf

SMART Criteria (2): Leonard, Kimberlee. Watts, Rob. (2024). The Ultimate Guide To S.M.A.R.T. Goals. https://www.forbes.com/advisor/business/smart-goals/

13 Feedforward: Goldsmith, Marshall. (2015). Try Feedforward Instead of Feedback. https://marshallgoldsmith.com/articles/try-feedforward-instead-feedback/

14 Carol Dweck: A Summary of Growth and Fixed Mindsets. (2015). https://fs.blog/carol-dweck-mindset/

Products

p1 Todoist. https://todoist.com

p2 Trello. https://trello.com

p3 Jira by Atlassian. https://www.atlassian.com/software/jira

p4 Microsoft To Do. https://to-do.office.com/tasks/

p5 Evernote. https://evernote.com

p6 Franklin Planner. https://store.franklinplanner.com

p7 Full Focus. https://fullfocusstore.com

p8 Time Doctor. https://www.timedoctor.com

p9 Toggl. https://toggl.com

p10 RescueTime. https://www.rescuetime.com

ABOUT THE AUTHOR

Steven Bradley

 Steven (Steve) Bradley is an expert in the field of technology and business management. And now an author. With years of experience leading teams to drive value in various industries, he brings a wealth of practical knowledge and insights to his writing. Throughout his career, Bradley has helped numerous individuals unlock their leadership potential and achieve success in their professional endeavors.